Retailing

The Insider Career Guides *is a dynamic series of books designed to give you the inside track on individual careers – how to get in, how to get on, even how to get out.*

Based on the real-life experiences of people actually working in these fields, each title offers a combination of hard practical information and insider information on working culture, the pros and cons of different areas of work, prospects for promotion, etc.

Other titles in the series:

Banking and the City
Karen Holmes

The Environment
Melanie Allen

Information and Communications Technology
Jacquetta Megarry

Sport
Robin Hardwick

Travel and Tourism
Karen France

About the Series Editor
Following a successful career as a teacher and lecturer in the UK and the Far East, Karen Holmes now works as a freelance writer, editor and project manager. Specialising in learning and careers, she has authored a range of careers literature for publishers and other commercial organisations.

Retailing

by

Liz Edwards

First published in 1999 by
The Industrial Society
Robert Hyde House
48 Bryanston Square
London W1H 7LN

© The Industrial Society 1999

ISBN 1 85835 578 8

**British Library Cataloguing-in-Publication Data.
A catalogue record for this book is available from the
British Library.**

Typeset by: The Midlands Book Typesetting Company
Printed by: Cromwell Press
Cover by: Sign Design
Cover image: Tony Stone

The Industrial Society is a Registered Charity No. 290003

CONTENTS

INTRODUCTION

So you want to work... in retailing? Whether you see yourself as a key mover in a superstore, the manager of a high street operation or the buyer for a fashion group, this is the book for you.

How do you find out about a career that interests you? If you want to research effectively, you would contact organisations that work in the relevant industry, look at recruitment literature and talk to the professionals, the people who already work there. That is just what we have done to prepare this series of books.

The Insider guides give you the inside story on what it is really like to work in a particular field of employment. These titles will help you to find out more about different professionals and their cultures, the day-to-day working routines, and the opportunities that exist for you.

In this title, *The Insider Career Guide to Retailing*, you will find useful information about:

- the retailing industry
- how to start your career
- what qualities employers are looking for in their new recruits
- opportunities for training and development
- promotion and the way to the top.

This book is divided into three sections:

Part One, *The Job*, gives you an up-to-date overview of the retailing industry, including:

- trends in recruitment
- what different sectors of the industry involve (do you know the difference between a convenience and a community store?)

- brief descriptions of individual areas of employment within some of the sectors
- an insight into the daily routine of some of the people who work in the industry
- the vital statistics – important details such as the qualifications and/or experience you need to get into retailing, how much you can expect to earn, and so on.

Part Two, *The Person*, focuses on some of the people who work in the industry. First, it gives a simple quiz which asks if you have the qualities that would let you succeed in the world of retailing. It then goes on to look at:

- the skills and experience successful recruits require
- the personal characteristics that will help you in the job
- inside information from people who work in the industry about their working lives.

Part Three, *Getting in, Getting on. . . Getting out* looks at:

- where you can find out about current vacancies
- how to make applications that catch the eye of company recruiters
- the training and development you will receive once you join the industry
- opportunities for promotion and advancement
- related careers – where do people who leave retailing go next?

No book can tell you everything you want to know. This is particularly so for retailing as it covers a wide spectrum, from the flower stall by the side of the road through specialist independents to the hypermarkets where 'one-stop shopping' is the aim. Whilst there are many 'frontline' roles, such as those who serve and manage operations in a wide variety of areas, there are also many other related areas – buying, merchandising, information technology, logistics, human resources and so on.

Once you have read *The Insider Career Guide to Retailing* you will probably want to carry out your own research, so we have supplied useful contact and website addresses where you can access more information. With checklists to help you plan your job search, case studies, quotes from industry professionals and 'myth busters' that address popular misconceptions about working life, you'll find plenty of inside information in these pages to start you on your chosen career path.

part one   **the job**

the job

Introduction

Maybe we are a nation of shopkeepers – or retailers, as they are known these days. If we are such a nation then, within that nation, there should be many opportunities for those starting out on their careers.

Retailing – a familiar word, and possibly a familiar area to you as a customer! However, as a customer, have you ever stopped to think about how much is involved in getting the products into the shops and onto the shelves ready for you to buy?

'Retailing consists of identifying a market, purchasing goods for resale to that market, distributing the goods, pricing, marketing and merchandising the products to meet the market's expectations and providing excellent customer service with the goods.'

Distributive National Training Organisation (DNTO)

As you can see, there are a lot of different elements involved in retailing – none of these can be serviced without the input and efforts of many people. But, how many people are we talking about? The retailing industry is one of the bigger occupational areas and represents approximately 10% of all those employed in the UK.

Retailing employees (including self-employed)

Total	Males	Females	Part-time	Full-time
2.7 million	39.4%	60.6%	50.4%	49.6%

Source: Labour Force Survey (Spring 1997)

But what of the future? The forecast (to the year 2006) is that there will be a substantial increase in those employed in retailing. However, the majority will be part time, including an increase in male part-timers (Institute of Economic Research, Warwick University).

This should be good news for anyone thinking about this industry for a career – whilst other occupation areas are declining, retailing should continue to expand.

Retailing changes

'It is more dynamic now – a manager is looked upon as being different. It is no longer "just working in a shop" but higher profile. There are more opportunities – particularly as a management entrant.'

Sales manager, department store

We have come a long way since Napoleon made his comment in the 19th century. There have been many changes to the industry – particularly in the last 30 years or so. Outlets now come in all shapes and sizes and cover all the customer's needs and wants – from food to luxury apparel.

Radical changes included the move to self-service and the birth of the supermarket. Then came more and bigger supermarkets with retailers being forced to look for out-of-town sites to fulfil their expansion ideas.

All over the country, large food stores and retail parks with a variety of outlets became part of the landscape and so 'one-stop shopping' was born. Shopping malls – incorporating a variety of large and small outlets alongside restaurants, leisure and entertainment facilities – were introduced from the USA. All these innovations led to a decline in the high street, with more and more small shops being forced to move to the malls, being taken over by multiple operators or closing down altogether.

Traditionally, retailing has been divided into two separate sectors – food and non-food. At one time, the only place you could get 'general provisions', such as bread, butter and the everyday staples of our diet, was in a specialist store selling groceries, meat or fish, etc. Now all these goods – and more

– can be found in a wide range of operations, from market stalls, through open-all-hours corner stores and petrol stations, to superstores and hypermarkets.

With the moving away from specialising into generalising, there has been a blurring of the edges between the two sectors.

> Most of the big food retailers – such as Safeway, Sainsbury's and Tesco – sell a wide range of non-food items. Marks & Spencer – primarily a clothing operation – has bakery, delicatessen, fresh meat and hot food counters, and continues to upgrade and repackage about 1,000 items in its food range each year.

Technological changes meant that stock control, ordering and taking customers' payments are simpler and quicker. Laser scanning has reduced pricing on individual items and automated stock control. Computer software has enabled retailers to gather more detailed sales and marketing data to get a better picture of customers' buying habits.

Electronic funds transfer (EFTPOS), which facilitates the immediate transfer of payments from customers' bank accounts, has made till transactions faster, but more importantly – with the increased use of credit cards – has reduced till fraud levels enormously.

The customer influence

Retailers used to decide what they would sell – what they thought their customers might buy! Things have changed; customers are now more demanding and retailing has become customer-driven.

> 'The customer is the king at the top – everyone underneath has to strive to ensure they keep the customer happy.'
> *Sales manager, department store*

Two reasons for this change are:

- the increasing levels of competition: more outlets with the same range of goods mean retailers are bidding for the same customers

- the Citizens' Charter (1991) led to customers developing clear expectations and demands about the goods, assistance and courtesy they should expect from retailers.

Retailers realised that excellence in customer care can be the difference between their success and failure.

> 'The customer doesn't have to shop with us – they have multiple choices about where they want to go and what they want to buy. We have to create the right environment, give them the best service and exceed their expectations to get them to return to us.'
>
> *Sales manager, department store*

So what changes did they make? First, they altered their view on customer service. Ten years or so ago, customer service was seen as important only for 'frontline staff' – sales assistants or anyone who dealt face to face with the buying public. Now retailers know that everyone, from the top down, has a responsibility for customer care.

> 'Everything is linked to the customer. Our chief executive stresses that we should be surprising customers and enhancing the service we give them. The customer service ethos must be more than just buzzwords.'
>
> *Training and development controller, department store*

Other changes included:

- stores opening up to 24 hours and for seven days a week
- making designer names more available to the public
- introducing more healthy and ready-to-eat food lines alongside specialist 'luxury' and ethnic ranges in food stores
- introducing 'added value' through offering crèches, bus collection and home delivery services.

What's what and who's who in retailing?

The retailing industry sells almost anything to you and me: food from all over the world; all the household gadgetry we should ever want; every colour, shape and style of garment to kit us from head to toe. These products are retailed through a variety of outlets, ranging from a couple of hundred to thousands of square feet in size. Before you plan a career in retailing, you need to have some idea about the variety of operations, the sectors to which they belong and some of the opportunities they offer.

In a book of this size, we can only give you an overview of the two main sectors (food and non-food) and highlight some of the categories and opportunities through brief case studies and quotes.

Retailing can be a minefield of jargon and acronyms. You may find it useful, therefore, to refer to the *Jargon buster* (page 75) when you read through the Guide.

THE FOOD SECTOR

Food retailing is made up of a number of groups, including major multiples, convenience stores, co-operatives and independents. The main bulk of the market is shared by the major multiples – Tesco, Sainsbury's, Safeway, etc.

Market share	Actual 1997	Projected 2005
The top ten multiples	63%	67%
Convenience	18%	18%
Co-operatives	7%	5%
Remainder	12%	10%
	£87 billion	£120 billion

These figures, coupled with the earlier forecast on employment, suggest that job opportunities might increase in the food industry.

The changing industry

Food retailing is a very exciting and dynamic industry with excellent career prospects for those who are prepared to work hard in this fast-moving consumer goods (fmcg) environment.

Although food retailing was slow to take up technology, it is rapidly preparing itself for the 21st century. Not only is laser scanning available in many operations, but 'do-it-yourself' scanning for customers, which saves them time queuing at checkouts, was introduced by Safeway and has been taken up by other multiples.

Other initiatives being looked at in conjunction with customers, advisers and the professional body, The Institute of Grocery Distribution (IGD), include supplementary nutrition labelling, packaging improvements and improving designs of stores to meet the needs of elderly and disabled customers. One major initiative – and the current buzzword in the food industry – is Efficient Consumer Response (ECR).

> 'A total industry initiative which aims to anticipate and meet consumer needs faster, better and with less cost. It focuses on improving efficiency and effectiveness in new product introductions, trade and consumer promotions, range and assortment and product replenishment.'
>
> *Institute of Grocery Distribution*

Let's now look at some of the players in food retailing.

The major multiples

Technically, a multiple is any operation with more than two stores trading. The major multiples, as their title indicates, operate many outlets in a range of sizes up to stores with 40,000sq. ft. of shopping and storage area.

> Tesco – currently no. 1 – has 600 stores in England, Scotland and Wales; Sainsbury's trades through more than 400, and Safeway has around 500 outlets. These three, along with Asda, shared 45% of the food retailing market in 1997.
>
> *Institute of Grocery Distribution*

The range is large and varied: not just English apples or Italian zabaglione, but exotic fruits from the Far East and traditional puddings from Middle Eastern countries. Their non-food range means a family can buy their clothes, videos and CDs as well as the equipment for viewing and listening. Of course, it doesn't stop there: you can also buy the cupboards to put the clothes in and, at the same time, arrange the finance to pay for the shopping.

More and more, the major multiples are turning their stores into better one-stop shopping outlets as they offer facilities such as petrol, photo processing, dry cleaning and restaurants.

> 'Customer loyalty is a thing of the past, so we have to ensure we can keep them coming back.'
>
> *Personnel director*

The same products can be found in most of the major multiples – they have to look for ways in which to 'add value' and keep customers returning. These include counter service for meat, fish and bread; incorporating pharmacies and crèches as well as loyalty cards, baby and animal clubs and customer banking.

Who works in the major multiples?

~ MYTH BUSTER ~

If you can't get a proper job, you can always work in a supermarket

'Before joining, I believed food retailing was a job where you didn't need many skills – you didn't need to be intelligent, it was the lower end of the market. Actually, when you come into a big company you appreciate how many skills it does need.'
Area training and recruitment manager

Retailing, and particularly food retailing, hasn't been seen as an ideal job and often people have ended up in it by accident rather than design.

'I didn't intend to stay – I was still looking around for an administration job – but really began to love the job, the atmosphere and working as part of a team.'

Store manager

Food retailing is exciting and has excellent career paths, particularly in the larger organisations. The variety of opportunities is enormous, depending on the size of the organisation.

As with all industries, retailing has a range of titles for the operational jobs in their stores, but generally they fall into the categories of:

- general assistants
- supervisors and department heads
- deputy and store managers
- qualified bakers, butchers or fishmongers
- visualisers and merchandisers
- caterers
- pharmacists.

The range of goods in some of the large stores is so wide that a number of general staff may be allocated to one department or section with a supervisor or department head. Deputy and store managers will be responsible for the day-to-day running of the store, including stock levels, sales, profitability and staff.

'I am the unofficial deputy to the store manager. I am responsible for 130 people (and this is not a big store). My role is to deliver the 'customer proposition' through running several departments. I cannot manage all the people, but I can manage the controllers who run those departments and that is the biggest part of my job. If they do their job well, the departments run smoothly.'

Customer service manager

Whilst many retailers have offered fresh bread and fish for some time, they are now going back to traditional methods of preparing fresh meat to order – all these areas need the specialist skills of qualified bakers, fishmongers and butchers.

As the large multiples extend their range of goods further into the non-food sector, the focus on areas such as clothes, household goods and leisure items means that display and merchandising 'experts' are also needed. Some of these staff can be 'grown' in-house. For example, a general assistant showing a flair for creating an effective display can be developed through learning on the job and by attending an appropriate training course.

Whilst many superstores and hypermarkets have had restaurants on their premises, many more are now incorporating pharmacies. These operations need trained catering staff and pharmacists.

> 'After my degree, I started working for a local high street chemist. After a while, I realised that the opportunities to progress were very limited. I am now a pharmacy manager in a superstore following a period gaining experience in all aspects of the store operation. If I wish to move into the broader area of store management, or a job in head office, I know that the chances are available to me. I am responsible for the day-to-day running of the pharmacy, supervising the staff, the sales, profit and, of course, dispensing medicines, including prescriptions. A large amount of my time is spent dealing with customers and giving them advice.'
>
> *In-store pharmacy manager, superstore*

'Behind-the-scenes' staffing includes:

- maintenance and security
- administration and personnel (human resources: HR)
- warehouse operations and delivery.

These operations are key as many stores are now open 24 hours and deliveries are arriving continuously. With the introduction of delivery services to customers: staff are also needed to supervise and progress this operation.

> 'I worked in a variety of departments in the supermarket before I transferred to the warehouse. I was promoted to supervisor quite quickly. I am responsible for overseeing all the deliveries and ensuring that all the security procedures are followed. Security is essential as this area is one where theft can happen quite easily – whether it is someone on the staff or a delivery driver trying to steal. I don't have to check each individual item – that is the responsibility of the relevant department head, but I do have to

check that the delivery documents tally with what actually comes in. If things aren't okay, then I have to speak to the distribution centre or the relevant supplier.

You have to put in more hours than you are contracted for, but everything has to be unloaded and stacked in the right place. You need to be committed, be quick on the uptake and, because we have so much perishable food coming in, you have to be prepared to work in cold conditions – all year long.'

Supervisor, supermarket

Maintenance staff are crucial (a large array of equipment and machinery is needed in the warehouse) to transport goods from warehouse to shop floor, to bundle and bind cardboard ready for recycling and to crush rubbish and waste. On the shop floor, freezer cabinets and dairy cabinets must be in top working order, and shelving, flooring and lighting must be A1.

Whilst all members of staff have a responsibility for security, in larger stores it is essential to have dedicated security staff for two reasons:

- stock losses, through staff and customer pilfering, can be extremely high
- staff and the public may need protection from aggressive or dangerous individuals.

Some operations have dedicated personnel people who are responsible, as part of the management team, for all issues related to staff members.

'I am responsible for the implementation of policies and procedures; I liaise with department heads on recruitment, induction and training and development, and – with the store management team – on staffing strategy. I also deal with the administration of payroll, sickness and holidays.'

Personnel officer, superstore

Stores don't function totally autonomously. Area managers, regional controllers and regional directors have responsibility for groups of stores or an area of the country. Their roles will vary, but will include responsibility for the profit of stores within their control. They are likely to be involved in target setting, disciplinary issues, store operational issues, meetings with store and other area management and strategic planning – amongst other things!

> 'The role has changed over the years. When I was a store manager, we lived in fear and trepidation of regional management visits. If they found something wrong, and they usually did, they shouted or lost their tempers on the shop floor. They were very dictatorial. That has all changed: our role now is much more facilitative – staff are not frightened when we visit – and anyone, no matter what level in the store, can discuss problems with us.'
>
> *Regional controller, supermarket*

The large multiples generally mastermind their operations from a head office with a variety of departments including:

- accounting and finance
- merchandising and buying
- logistics
- food technology and product testing
- human resources
- information technology (IT) – management information and computer systems.

On their Internet websites:

- Safeway has advertised for people in a range of areas, including logistics, business development, property and development and finance.
- Tesco has been looking for a variety of IT specialists, such as analysts, programmers, trainers and support consultants.

Co-operative societies

Co-operatives societies are stores that have been around for many years – they are owned by the members and can be either independent or multiple operations. Well-known multiples include CWS (Co-operative Wholesale Society Limited) and CRS (Co-operative Retail Services Limited). Competition from other sectors has reduced market share and the trend is likely to continue downwards – from 7% in 1997 to 5% by the year 2005 (IGD).

Convenience stores

Convenience ('C') stores are 'small stores selling a wide but shallow mix of products, but predominately food and drink' (IGD). They offer customers a source for regular daily, top-up or emergency purchases. 'C' stores may be single units, small multiples or part of a petrol operation. Many of these who supply a general grocery range may be members of a symbol group – Spar, Londis; a confectionery, tobacco and newsagents (CTN) chain such as Dillons; or an off-licence chain such as Unwins. Their size – 300 to 3,000sq. ft. – means they are not restricted by Sunday trading laws and can trade for up to 24 hours seven days a week.

> 'Convenience-style stores is a group that is likely to grow in the future.'
>
> *DNTO*

Planning guidelines now restrict the development of out-of-town sites. The focus for large retailers on where and how they operate has changed and will continue to change. They are:

- reinvesting in the high streets through convenience-style stores, such as Sainsbury's 'Local'
- expanding their operations in petrol station forecourts, selling anything from car oil to hot coffee and pasties. This is one of the biggest areas of expansion, with Esso Snack, Shell Select and Tesco Express
- introducing the 'Community' store: city centre stores designed to meet specific customers' needs at different times of the day. This is an innovative format likely to become a big growth area, and includes Tesco's 'Metro' and Sainsbury's 'Central'.

Independents

The independents generally operate in specialist areas, such as greengrocery, butchery and poultry. Many independents have weathered the storm of competition from the multiples as many customers still prefer the personal service they can get at a small, independent store. The alcohol importation rules between the European mainland and the UK have threatened some wine independents. Many are being swallowed up by the multiples and have frequently been turned into off-licence-based convenience chains, such as those operated by Unwins.

One area that has expanded is 'niche' specialists, such as delicatessens, health food and ethnic food shops.

It is thought by some in this sector that the return of the multiples to the high streets may not necessarily be a threat. They believe they can operate more successfully alongside multiples as they serve a complementary market.

Who works in other food retailing groups?

Opportunities *do* exist with other food retailers. Many of these operations are small or specialist so the range of jobs is smaller and progression more limited.

Many independents may have only one or two part-time assistants and a manager. The work may be more varied with more responsibility than in a large store. This makes the job more interesting and gives individuals the chance to carry out a wide variety of tasks.

'I am a general assistant in a superstore working in the 'ambient' area – grocery, wines and spirits, videos, CDs and the cigarette kiosk. My role is to check and replenish stock. Although I do answer customers' queries as well, I do get a bit bored with doing the same things all the time.'

Assistant, superstore

'I work in a high street shop – there is just the manager, another part-timer and me. I do anything that needs doing, from telephoning head office for special orders to preparing window displays and, of course, talking to and serving customers. There is certainly plenty of variety.'

Sales assistant, variety store

Store managers in smaller operations may be less restricted by corporate procedures and policies. They can offer a greater range of responsibilities and duties.

By now, you should have some idea of the operations in the food side of retailing. Let's now look at the non-food sector.

THE NON-FOOD SECTOR

This sector has all those operations where the primary range is something other than food – from an abacus to a zoom lens, from a hat to shoes, and everything in between. Confusingly, many operations have diversified into food as well.

Non-food retailers can be independents or multiples operating mixed goods, department or specialist stores.

Mixed goods (variety stores)

Mixed goods stores are so called because they may sell anything from household equipment to cosmetics, clothes and confectionery. Mixed goods stores – independents and multiples – are located mainly in cities, the high street and shopping malls.

> • As well as retailing clothing, lighting and linens, Bhs runs in-store restaurants and offers snack food.
> • Marks & Spencer falls into this category, although it is primarily a clothing multiple.

Operators continually review their ranges and operations to keep abreast of customer demands and trends.

> Woolworth's is adapting its stores to 'Heartland', 'City Centre' and 'Local', with different identities and merchandise to meet the local customer market.

'Retailers are continuing to diversify the range of products on offer to increase their market share. They no longer sit comfortably in the tight sub-sectors they have been used to in the past.'

DNTO

If this sector is one that does expand, then there will be more opportunities for flexible people who can take change in their stride.

Who works in mixed goods stores?

Roles will be similar to those available in the large food retailers: general assistant to store managers as well as buying and merchandising staff. The balance of staff will be different depending on the focus of the organisation and the needs of the operations.

- Woolworth's employs around 31,000 staff in a variety of jobs, from sales assistants to senior managers and directors.
- Alongside management training schemes for school and college leavers, graduates and career changers, the Marks & Spencer organisation recruits for a variety of specialist areas, from bakery and butchery through lingerie and tailoring to window dressing and wines advising.

'After my children started school, I did an art course and got a job as a trainee visual merchandiser.

I am responsible for an area of the graphics and point of sale materials (POS) for the stores. My maturity helped me to adapt quickly and understand the importance of listening and learning from others. The pace is lively and the department is fun. I work in a team and we know the stores depend on us to make sure they are "kitted out" properly.'

Visual merchandiser, multiple store

Department stores

Debenhams opened the first department store in London nearly 200 years ago. Department stores are located on the high street in many towns, as well as being 'anchor' stores in the newer shopping malls, and include the John Lewis Partnership, House of Fraser and Allders.

Department stores have a large floor space, usually on a

number of floors, selling anything from clothing and household items to stationery, toys, games and cosmetics and perfumes. They sell own label goods and have sections franchised to such well-known names as Christian Dior, Esteé Lauder, Windsmoor and First Sport. They have some self-service sections, but most areas remain assisted with staff available for consultation and advice and a one-to-one service.

Department stores are meeting the customer challenge in a number of ways. Many offer discounts, special shopping evenings and previews to holders of their own storecards. Some have introduced 'personal shoppers' – staff who are available should a customer want extra advice or assistance.

> 'I had a customer who wanted an outfit for her daughter's wedding. I started by doing her "colours" – identifying which ones would look best with her colouring – and then she gave me an idea of what she wanted. I then picked out some alternatives and accessories.
>
> I was back and forth to the dressing room and up and down from one department to another, but she was delighted with the personal shopping service and I had fun helping her to choose. The best bit is that I know she went away extremely satisfied.'
>
> *Personal shopping assistant, department store*

Who works in department stores?

Department stores employ a wide range of people depending on the size of operation. The jobs will be similar to those identified for the large food multiples, although job titles and roles may differ slightly. General assistants may be allocated to one department, or could move around the store on a day-to-day basis, depending on the need.

> 'When I first started as an assistant, I reported to personnel who would send me to whichever department needed me. After a few months of moving around, I was allocated to children's wear which was short-staffed – that became my first permanent post.'
>
> *Sales manager, department store*

Other opportunities exist in back up operations either in-store or at head office.

The Debenhams management trainee programme has opportunities in a number of areas including:

- **Systems (information)** supporting the business by 'providing flexible, cost-efficient systems designed to enhance our profitability and growth'.
- **Catering/food services** offering high quality, value-for-money ranges from coffee shops to restaurants.

'My job is to promote the management training programme and careers in the organisation. I communicate with university careers services, technical colleges and schools so they know what is available. I also make sure our various publications are up to date and on the Internet. I make presentations, write materials and do the public relations.'

Recruitment manager, department store

Specialist retailing

This covers a wide range of operations, including fashion stores, do-it-yourself (DIY), furniture, electrical goods and bookshops.

Fashion stores

Fashion stores range from independents of one 'boutique' to more familiar multiple operations – selling primarily clothing and footwear.

- The Arcadia group focuses on difference audiences with fashion outlets, including Burtons Menswear, Dorothy Perkins and Principles.
- Mothercare (Storehouse group) sells children and babies clothing and equipment.

Stores are located in the high street, city centres, shopping malls, and can be franchises within department stores. Many fashion stores expect their staff to be able to give advice and make suggestions for customers.

Fashion stores are more likely to be affected when the economic outlook is gloomy as customers reduce their outlay on fashion before they cut back on food. Stores located in tourist areas may also be affected if the pound sterling is strong: visitors stay away and stores lose trade.

'I manage our store in London's West End. Working here is quite different to other areas in the country. Whilst I have to recruit staff who are good with customers, they also need to appreciate different cultures and, if possible, be able to speak a foreign language. We have lots of visitors from overseas — many of whom cannot speak or have very little English. We always know when tourism is doing well because our store trades better.'

Store manager, ladies fashions

Household goods

Household goods can be sold in anything from a small store to a multiple. Many of the bigger operations are located in retail parks and other out-of-town locations selling furniture, carpets, electrical goods and textiles. When people started getting involved in DIY — tackling decorating and re-vamping rooms — there was a huge growth in the number of large outlets selling tools and materials, as well as all the kitchen, bedroom and bathroom fittings needed for people's 'new' hobbies. This led to a reduction in traditional hardware shops and the influx of multiples such as B&Q and Do It All.

Computer stores

Computer stores range from small high street shops to superstore multiples such as the Dixon group's PC World. However, possibly because of the professional advice usually available to new users in independent stores, many of these continue to thrive, despite the competition from the multiples and mail order operations.

Booksellers and stationers

This category includes Dillons and Waterstones. WH Smith Retail is primarily a bookseller, but can be classed as a 'mixed goods' operation because of its diverse range. Branches are found mainly in the high street and shopping malls. Office World and Staples — specialists stationery superstores — are located in a mixture of out-of-town and urban sites.

The introduction of a free pricing regime has meant that multiples are able to sell books more competitively than independent stores. This, coupled with American bookstores starting to operate in the UK, has had a great impact, particularly on the independents. Those independents which have survived are either located in small towns and city suburbs, or have specialised in subject matters such as sport, cookery or religion. If they are to survive, others may have to broaden their range of goods or offer customer benefits such as children's play areas, in-store coffee shops and 'browsing' areas.

Chemists and druggists

This sector includes opticians and dedicated cosmetic stores. Multiple operators are Boots Chemists, Lloyds, Superdrug (the Kingfisher Group), SpecSaver and Boots Opticians. Independent chemists have been hit by the introduction of pharmacies into the large multiple food operations and are likely to continue to decline.

Other specialists

Specialists include 'niche' retailers, such as jewellers, sporting goods, craft and gift stores and pet shops, as well as mail order, charity shops and market trading.

Home shopping has increased by more than 40% between 1993 and 1997 (Chartered Institute of Marketing). Operators such as Littlewoods, Freemans and Grattan are losing market shares to multiples and 'niche' specialists such as Windrush (gardening), Art Room (fine art) and Lakeland limited (household storage and kitchenware). Home shopping is likely to continue to expand with electronic commerce (purchases through TV view data) and, as more retailers develop their websites, increasing numbers of customers will shop via the Internet.

> Tesco was the first UK retailer to offer Internet-based home shopping.

Who works in specialist retailing?

The range of people who work in these areas will depend, to a great extent, on the size of the operation. Besides opportunities from sales assistant to management, there should also be possibilities for those with a specialist skill or who want to follow a hobby. If you have a keen interest in sport, you may want to look at a sports shop such as ActiveVenture or First Sport (JJB Sports group). But, remember, you must also want to work with customers!

> 'I have always loved books and reading and, as I am an active member in my local church, I was able to get a job in The Bookworm. I am now supervisor in the non-Christian section. I have gained great knowledge on different religions as well as a lot of experience in customer service. With my new role, I am responsible for one part-timer, so I am learning about managing and training staff.'
>
> *Bookstore supervisor*

VITAL STATISTICS

You should be getting an idea of the size of the retailing industry as well as an overview of the some of the different types of operations in the industry. This information gives you a picture of the possibilities that could be open to you. There are many different career opportunities – the choice is wide and deep.

> Sainsbury's employs nearly 122,000 people; Safeway has more than 75,000 employees; and Woolworth's has 31,300 people working for it.

> 'In Debenhams, we have more than 18,000 jobs in our department stores and approximately another 1,500 in head office. You might be a finance manager, the guy who buys escalators for the new stores or a retailer on the shop floor.'
>
> *Training and development co-ordinator, department store*

Retailing, unlike many others, is one industry where the entry requirements are fairly open. Getting on, however, is different – you can progress, but you must have commitment above all.

'Retailing is a very open career – you don't always have to have a great academic background to get on. I had no formal qualifications: I now run my own branch of a leading fashion store with a staff of 40. I love my job and get enormous satisfaction from achieving targets, pleasing customers and developing my staff.'

Store manager, ladies fashion

If you leave school with a minimum of qualifications (two GCSEs or equivalent) you can enter as a general assistant. (This job could also be titled sales assistant/consultant/advisor or associate.) Salaries start at around £3 per hour, depending on age and experience. (The minimum wage has been set at £3.60 per hour for adults and £3 for those aged 18–21.) Benefits depend on the organisation, and the sector, but they could include: discounts, subsidised restaurants, sales commissions, bonuses and non-contributory pensions. If you have to wear a uniform then this will be supplied.

A day in the life...

I had four GCSEs and a Saturday job in a coffee shop. I liked talking to people and I was interested in clothes, so I joined a fashion store as a YTS trainee – after six months I was taken on full time, continued my NVQ in retailing (levels 1 and 2) and was made footwear manager.

I started here as a general assistant when the store opened. I now manage my own sales team and am training to be an NVQ assessor. Whilst the wages are not good, particularly when you start, the benefits are. If you want to get on, you need to be career minded, work hard and be committed.

I work shifts: on the early one, I have to open up, set up till, work out staffing rotas for the day and carry out team briefings. I control 'write-offs' – faulty garments customers bring back which are sent to charity – and I make sure that the hangers are properly recycled. Serving customers takes up a big percentage of my time – between 11am and 3pm we focus completely on the customer.

If I do the late shift from 12 noon to 9pm, I am responsible for cashing up all the tills and following the store closing procedures – checking the exits, testing locks and making sure that everyone has left the store.

The hours are getting longer, and if I could change anything it would be these. I find the run up to Christmas particularly difficult

(continued overleaf)

because the store is open until 10pm. I have a long journey so I am often not home until midnight. The only other problem is the odd moaning customer!

Supervisor, ladies' fashion

If you want to join retailing and have A levels (or the equivalent), there is a variety of options available. You could enter as a general assistant and work your way up. A number of organisations have retail schemes for those with A levels, or the equivalent, or with previous experience. Salaries will depend on the organisation and the scheme, but for a school or college leaver they are likely to be between £11,000 and £15,000. Benefits will vary, but may include many of those identified previously, as well as private health care, sharesave options and interest-free loans.

'I joined the management training scheme straight from school with two A levels. Whilst I was at school I had a Saturday job and got interested in a career in food retailing. The competition was very fierce to get on to the scheme despite the fact that I was working for them already.

Following an induction with the other trainees at head office to learn all about the company, policies and procedures, the law and operations, I had a period of job shadowing in two different stores. Now I am in my base store where I am learning about different aspects of the store, how to run a department and how to apply all the policies and procedures. I have a mentor to whom I go if I have any queries or difficulties with any aspect of the programme, but, of course, I also have the store manager and my department head to turn to.

I will be attending another off-job training and assessment week shortly. I am hoping, if all goes well there, to get my own departmental responsibilities after that.

I am very pleased I joined the scheme – the work is hard, but the atmosphere is exciting and ever changing. If you aren't prepared to work hard and don't like people, then don't do it! You will get out what you put in – and I am prepared to put in lots.'

Management trainee

If you are in your gap year, a graduate or a post graduate, there are opportunities either to get a 'taster' of what retailing is all about, or to get on a fast-track management training scheme. Starting salaries on management training schemes range between £16,000 and £20,000 (1998). Head office functions are likely to start on a higher rate than retailing, and information technology attracts the highest salary. Benefits will be as similar to those for staff at other levels.

'I didn't have a clue what I wanted to do after I graduated. I was working in retail as a stop gap and I really, really enjoyed it. It is quite a reactive environment, fairly hectic and with loads of variety. However, although I am a 'people' person, I didn't want a retail post: I wanted to work in human resources.

I spent the first six months of my training in the HR department finding out what it was all about and working on job-related projects. I then spent six months in a store learning about how it operates, working with the HR team and administering all aspects of the department, such as recruitment, induction, terms and conditions and job descriptions. I assisted with interviews and disciplinary and grievance procedures. I gained an incredible insight as to how the human resources function operates at store level and the reactive nature of the roles in that function.

I returned to head office for the remainder of my training. During this time I had to complete a project: an update on policy and procedure for stores. I also attended various training programmes and had regular assessments with my tutor.

I have just started my first appointment dealing with all HR aspects of the millennium. Any queries from the field or head office about Y2K (year two thousand) come to me. Believe me, they are many and varied.'

Human resources assistant, department store

If you want a career change, either from one sector to another or from outside the industry, there are opportunities to do this. If you go into a supervisory or department head role, the rate of pay will depend on the organisation, the sector and your previous experience, but may start at around £17,000. If you join a management training scheme, the rates could be higher.

A day in the life...

My first career – as a teacher – meant I was experienced in working with people. Retail needs those who have more of a natural desire to help people much more than a technical knowledge – the company provides the technical side.

I am responsible for the people improvement progress within the stores in my area. I don't have an average week – two-thirds of my time is in stores meeting people or running training sessions. The remainder is planning training, reviewing what the area needs, evaluating training and recruiting management trainees. I manage succession plans and making sure stores are doing everything possible for their human resource.

My philosophy is, 'Let's look at how we can get it better.' I have no line manager accountability but am very much the persuader and influencer. I need to get job satisfaction from working with people rather than hanging my hat on results – these come through very slowly over years as I see the improvement.

I can work double my contracted hours but it is my own fault as I am my own boss. I cover 16 stores and, because store hours have extended. I may be visiting early in the morning or late in the evening. On average, I probably do about 55 hours. On the other hand, if I feel I have done too much, I can take time off in lieu.

I enjoy meeting people, the flexibility and the freedom – I have complete control over my own diary. I don't like it if I have to change direction at short notice. This could happen through a new initiative or if the financial results are not as good as the company wants them to be. They suddenly say, 'Change/cancel the training planned for the next three months.' I then have to think about getting results in a different way. Coping with this is part and parcel of retail – you have to have the temperament and you must be very flexible. This doesn't mean you roll over all the time – you do put your point of view – but if the message is, 'Sorry, we have to go in that direction,' you have to accept it. Otherwise you drive yourself into an early grave.

I can apply for any job within my grade that has similar competencies. The prospects are there for me if I want them. I am not ambitious, partly because of my age and partly because you need to be careful not to overstretch yourself – poor performance is not tolerated. You need to be very careful if going for promotion that you are going to be able to manage it.

Area training and recruitment manager, superstore

A day in the life...

I was self-employed as a painter and decorator. I wanted a change and a friend told me about a vacancy for a security officer. Although I had no qualifications or relevant experience, I must have impressed because I got the job. When my manager opened this store, she asked me to join as security manager.

My manager's motto for us is, 'The best minute I spend is the one I invest in people.' She is right – although I am not officially a retailer, I have to be able to deal with people in different ways – staff, customers, shoplifters, executives. I have to be dedicated as the job demands a lot. Officially I work a 39-hour week, but usually do about 45 hours to meet the needs of the business.

On an average day, I check the camera system, oversee the store security – back door, staff and key control. I also do a sort of auditing job on the cash office; checking the banking and safe, and doing spot checking on the tills. We have management meetings every week.

I enjoy getting results and that usually means arresting people such as a dishonest member of staff or a shoplifter. That's what I am here for – to keep stock losses down.

Security manager, supermarket

Obviously, there is no one person who is perfect for retailing, but there are some skills and attributes that are more appropriate if you want a career in this industry. Let's now look at the 'retailing person'.

part two   the person

the person

Introduction

> 'Those who work in retailing must have a number of skills, but above all, they must like people. People are the focus of everything – in both the food and non-food sectors.'
>
> *Human resources director*

Is retailing really for you? If so, should you work in food or would you be better in non-food? Have you always fancied yourself as the chairman of a supermarket chain or as the next Richard Branson introducing new innovations in fashion retailing? What sort of person do you think you are and, more importantly, do you think you have what is needed to help you get on if you do decide on a career in retailing?

This section should enable you to answer some of the above questions. It gives you a mini-audit, designed to help you reflect on some of the skills and attributes that have been identified as essential for those who work in retailing. You can make your own mind up as to whether you might be a round or a square peg in a round hole.

Once you have done that, it goes on to give you some brief comments from 'insiders' as to the skills they feel they had to have, or needed to develop, to work in the industry.

WHAT SORT OF PERSON WORKS IN RETAILING?

> 'Are you free, Mr Humphries?'

Although the sit-com *Are You Being Served?* gave an exaggerated view of retailing, it probably had some basis in how retailing operated some years ago. Things have changed since then: so what does that mean for those who might want to work in the industry?

MYTH BUSTER

You don't need any particular skills to work in retailing

Not true! Retailing now is a dynamic, fast-moving industry. It looks for people who can move and react with the times and the demands made on them. They need to:

- be prepared to work hard
- work effectively as part of a team
- take pride in what they do
- be willing to get on with whatever task is put before them.

'Anyone who works for us must be prepared to work hard and understand that this business is customer-driven. Also, whilst we expect our people to be proactive, they have to be able to react to situations and solve problems.'

Recruitment manager, department store

So, are you right for retailing? Let's find out. The following test shouldn't be taken too seriously; it just gives you the opportunity to see whether some of your skills and attitudes are suitable for retailing. Do you like people? Do you pay attention to detail? Do you prefer to work alone or with others? What do you know about retailing?

Read through each multiple-choice question and tick the box that most applies to you.

Are you right for retailing?

1. When I am out with friends:
    a. I find it difficult to put forward my viewpoint ☐
    b. they don't always understand what I have to say ☐
    c. they usually listen to what I have to say ☐
    d. they ignore me when I am putting forward my opinions. ☐

2. I think working in a team:
   a. means you may not get credit for what you do ☐
   b. is unnecessary if you can do your job properly ☐
   c. is better for those in the team and the customers ☐
   d. is important only for team sports. ☐

3. If someone criticises me, I usually:
   a. give them as good as I get ☐
   b. try to find out what the problem is ☐
   c. get very upset ☐
   d. don't take any notice. ☐

4. ECR is an acronym for:
   a. Economic Community Retailers ☐
   b. Efficient Customer Response ☐
   c. Elderly Cats Register ☐
   d. Electrical Creditors Range. ☐

5. I like work where:
   a. someone gives me clear directions and instructions ☐
   b. I can make things happen ☐
   c. there are people around me who will motivate me ☐
   d. I don't have to make decisions. ☐

6. If an organisation is categorised as a 'multiple', it means it:
   a. operates units with a number of floors ☐
   b. sells a variety of goods ☐
   c. has a minimum of two stores trading similarly ☐
   d. has a number of stores. ☐

7. If I see someone with luggage or a pushchair struggling to tackle some stairs, I:
   a. pretend I haven't noticed them ☐
   b. trip them up as I go past ☐

   c. smile, say something like, 'That's a handful you have there,' and pass on ☐

   d. offer to assist. ☐

8. Verbal communication is important:

   a. only when you need something done ☐

   b. for anyone working in a team ☐

   c. only if you have to work in the 'frontline' with customers ☐

   d. just for social occasions – too many people talk too much! ☐

9. EFTPOS is a method for:

   a. scanning items to check prices ☐

   b. registering customers' purchases at the checkout ☐

   c. obtaining customers' money direct from their bank accounts ☐

   d. searching customers' bags before they leave the store. ☐

10. People in teams:

   a. only need to meet when there are problems ☐

   b. should be allowed to get on with their own job in their own way ☐

   c. should be united and work towards a group objective ☐

   d. thrive on conflict – it makes them stronger than other teams. ☐

11. A barcode is:

   a. a security number on a product ☐

   b. a code to get you into a members-only club ☐

   c. the vertical stripe on a product which identifies it ☐

   d. used to identify food items. ☐

12. If I am asked to make decisions:

   a. I gather all the information no matter how long it takes ☐

   b. I make them quickly – I can always change my mind later ☐

   c. I try to weigh up the advantages and disadvantages ☐

   d. I panic and ask someone else! ☐

13. Frontline staff are:

    a. those who work on the customer service desk ☐

    b. those who get shot first! ☐

    c. all staff who deal directly with customers ☐

    d. staff who have to deal with customer complaints. ☐

14. I believe the best people for retail are those who:

    a. are able to take risks and don't conform ☐

    b. push for recognition and what they deserve ☐

    c. are able to work with others ☐

    d. know who's in charge and will do what that person says. ☐

15. If I am in a heated discussion, I:

    a. like to butt in to give my opinion ☐

    b. listen before I give my opinion ☐

    c. make sure I get my views in first ☐

    d. try to agree with everyone to calm things down. ☐

16. I am usually:

    a. happier when I am by myself ☐

    b. not bothered about those around me ☐

    c. considered to be 'pushy' when I am with people ☐

    d. interested in meeting people. ☐

17. If I have a project/task to do, I usually:

    a. rush into it, make lots of mistakes but complete it in a fashion ☐

    b. spend too much time thinking about it ☐

    c. do it well but miss the deadline ☐

    d. complete it within the timescales. ☐

18. A store is classed as 'convenience' because it:

    a. sells a range of goods, but mainly hot snacks ☐

    b. is located close to new housing estates ☐

    c. sells a range of goods, but mainly food and drink ☐

    d. has toilets attached to it. ☐

19. If things don't go right, I usually:

     a. get annoyed and take it out on others   ☐

     b. feel it is someone else's fault   ☐

     c. just shrug and accept it   ☐

     d. try to learn from my mistakes.   ☐

20. I want a job:

     a. in a quiet environment   ☐

     b. where there is a buzz   ☐

     c. where I don't have to stand up for long   ☐

     d. where the pace is fairly even.   ☐

21. Unless you are a manager, you should:

     a. not have to work long hours   ☐

     b. work overtime only if you get paid for it   ☐

     c. do as little as possible   ☐

     d. be committed to getting the job done.   ☐

22. Customer loyalty:

     a. is a thing of the past so retailing can't do anything about it   ☐

     b. can be improved if retailers give customers better service   ☐

     c. comes naturally if a retailer sells quality goods   ☐

     d. can be achieved with reduced prices and special offers.   ☐

23. I want a job:

     a. that gives me loads of money for little effort   ☐

     b. with some variety, but I don't like interruptions   ☐

     c. that is flexible and challenging   ☐

     d. that has a clear routine – I need to know where I am.   ☐

24. I would like to be a manager because:

     a. I enjoy telling others what to do   ☐

     b. I could run a store the way I want to   ☐

     c. people would look up to me   ☐

     d. I could influence those around me.   ☐

How did you do? The majority of the questions don't have a right or wrong answer: only one that is more appropriate if you think you want to work in retailing.

Questions: 1c; 8b and 15b.

Good communication is essential in retailing. You don't need to be an impressive orator but you do need to be able to express yourself clearly, listen effectively and use appropriate body language.

> 'A lot of what I do is about talking to people – I need to be able to speak easily and relate to others.'
>
> *Senior sales, ladies' fashion*

> 'You need to be a good communicator as 90% of the communication is by mouth – despite the amount of paperwork we get these days.'
>
> *Sales manager, department store*

Questions: 2c; 10c; 14c and 24d.

Retailing and teamwork go hand in hand: an effective team that works together can achieve more than the individuals could if they work on their own. Teams are crucial to the day-to-day running and development of retail operations. Team members must be prepared to work together – whatever level they are – to contribute to the team goals as well as to the organisational goals.

> 'It is very lively but at times quite pressurised so I put a lot of effort into team motivation. Everything doesn't always go according to plan – and it is essential that we all work together.'
>
> *Regional manager, ladies' fashion*

Of course, if you are hoping to get into retailing as a manager or on to a management training scheme, then you will be expected to demonstrate leadership skills. Teams need someone who is able to lead by example and motivate the members.

'I have had a really good track record with staff who have worked in my team in the past. I like to think they have taken on some of my views and ideas. Many are now managers themselves. "Lead by example" is my motto.'

Sales manager, department store

Questions: 3b; 17d and 19d.

Personal effectiveness encompasses a variety of skills: being flexible, adapting to situations around you, making a positive impact and being able to learn from your mistakes. It is also about having self-confidence and behaving assertively.

'Dealing with awkward customers can be very difficult. It is important to keep calm and behave in a non-aggressive manner – particularly when they are wrong!'

Sales manager designate, department store

'When I was on the training scheme, there were so many challenges and I made lots of errors. I learned a lot from my mistakes and always asked for help if I wasn't certain how I needed to change my behaviour.'

Ex-graduate trainee, department store

Questions: 5b; 12c; 20b; 21d and 23c.

Retailing is not an easy option: the work is demanding, the pace is frenetic and the hours can be long. But it is also an exciting environment. If you have ever been in a food supermarket, particularly towards the end of the week, or in a department or fashion store near Christmas, you will understand. Staff have to think (and stay) on their feet, work long hours, be consistently pleasant to the customers and deal with problems as they happen.

'You need to put in the hours to meet the needs of the business. My contract says 38 hours but I have to be flexible and work, on average, about 45 hours.'

Security manager, supermarket

In some outlets, or in a head office, the pace may not be as fast but it will still be demanding.

'You need to be someone who likes challenge and variety because every day is different. You have to enjoy working in a team environment and you mustn't mind some anti-social hours.'
Customer services manager, superstore

Questions: 7d; 16d and 22b.
In Part One *The Job*, we stressed that retailing is customer-driven. If you want a retail job, then you will need to be interested in customers. You will have to appreciate their needs and try to meet them, however difficult this may be.

Did you know...
Customer loyalty and lifetime value can be worth up to ten times as much as the price of a single purchase. It costs up to six times more to attract new customers than to keep old ones!

'If you work in retail you must have enthusiasm and drive and like people – whether you work in a store or head office. If you are working on the shop floor you have to really enjoy dealing with customers, be prepared to work hard and do anything.'
Training and development controller, department store

Questions:
4b.
Efficient Customer Response is an initiative of the food industry – if you want to remind yourself about it, flip back to page 8.

6c.
Technically, a multiple is any operation with more than two stores trading similarly.

9c.
Electronic Funds Transfer Point of Sale is the computer operating system for 'taking' a customer's money from their bank account instantly when they use a debit card – such as Switch or Delta – to pay for their purchases.

11c.
A barcode is the black and white label on a product. Scanners read it to identify the product and price.

13c.
Whilst frontline staff do operate on the customer service desk, and probably often feel they are getting shot, they are any staff who deal with customers.

18c.
A 'C' store was defined in full on page 14.

If you go for an interview with a retailing organisation, you will not be expected to know everything about the industry, but you do need to have some awareness of how it operates.

> 'Before I attended my interview, I went to my local library to find out what I could about retailing and the company I was going to. I used the Internet to get into various websites: from these I learned quite a bit about the food industry and the company. I hadn't realised the organisation was so big and I got an insight into the size of the operation, their finances as well as their history.'
>
> *Ex-graduate trainee, department store*

Whilst there are some basic skills needed for retailing, there are others that are desirable depending on what it is you want to do and how high up the ladder you want to climb.

> 'I believe the attributes I need are drive, the desire to get results, intellectual curiosity, an understanding of how people and organisations operate and a knowledge of training and development.'
>
> *Training and development controller, department store*

'I feel that the skills I needed most, whilst on the graduate training scheme, were flexibility, resilience and tenacity. There were times when I had to hang on in there. I also felt that my ability to watch and learn assisted me, and is helping me now whilst I am in my first post. I think anyone who comes into retailing needs to be able to adapt, take the rough with the smooth and enjoy the reactive nature of the work, the pressure and the variety.'

Personnel officer, department store head office

One final, key point: if you are a fanatic about a team sport and look forward to spending your weekends running around a pitch, then you will need to take a long, hard look at what you want to do. Many areas of retailing have unsociable hours with different leisure times to the majority of the population – and this leisure time can vary from week to week. Retailing doesn't have too many 9-5 jobs!

'I think my biggest bugbear is the hours – they are getting longer and longer and, of course, we are now open seven days a week. I either have to work the early shift from 7am to 4pm, or the late from noon to 9pm, but, of course, these change at busy times such as the run-up to Christmas and the January sales.'

Senior sales, ladies' fashion

On the other hand, for some it can be a distinct advantage to work some unusual shift patterns.

'I don't work abnormal hours but they are not rigid office hours – we are at the "sharp end" of the business after all. It does give me a lot of time with my family and this was particularly good when my children were small. It also means my social life is so much easier. During the week, I can have a round of golf or go to the sports centre without too many other people around.'

Customer services manager, superstore

So, if you are still convinced that retailing is for you, carry on...

part three

getting in, getting on...
getting out

getting in, getting on... getting out

Introduction

Are you getting a clearer picture of some of the opportunities and whether you and retailing might be good for each other? The third, and final, part of this *Insider Career Guide* should help you to make your mind up. It focuses on the practicalities of how you can:

- get into the industry
- move up the career ladder
- approach making a change and moving into a new field of employment – if you want to.

MYTH BUSTER

Anyone can get a job in retailing

Make no mistake: the job market is highly competitive. And whilst retailing has a breadth of opportunities, you shouldn't think it is an easy option. At one time, organisations received few replies to job adverts; these days the response to some advertised posts could be well into the hundreds – and that is just for one vacancy.

'If I could change anything it would be some of the people – there are too many doing the job who shouldn't be doing it. People come into retail because they feel it is an easy place to get into and it is just a job – a stop gap. I want people to be in it because they want to be in it. Making a career in retail is just as important as a career in science.'

Sales manager, department store

How can you make your application stand out from the rest? A little insider knowledge can go a long way towards helping you prepare an application that will be noticed. Then, if you are invited to an interview, you can improve your chances by being prepared, understanding what the selectors are looking for and performing well.

Once you have found the job you think you want, how will your career take shape after that? What prospects are there for advancement? We look at how you can climb the career ladder, the opportunities for training and development, and follow some of the paths established employees have taken.

Finally, if, after a period in the retailing sector, you decide that you want to move on to something new, the experience and skills you have gained in retailing could prove invaluable in other industries. Which areas of employment should you be targeting next?

Read on to find out.

GETTING IN

Where do you start?

If you are still in education, or are thinking about this area for the first time, you need to know how best to research which retailer does what, where they do it and what is available for potential recruits. After all, retailing is a huge industry with an amazing number of possibilities. Should you consider food or fashion; should you work in logistics or buying; or should you target a multiple or independent? Where will you find out?

Career services: schools, colleges and universities have dedicated career offices where you can get advice, pick up literature or borrow books. The local careers service can provide independent, impartial guidance – your nearest branch should be in the telephone directory. They may be useful, particularly if you are leaving school with reasonable GCSEs and want to get a job but continue with your education. They should have details of any retail Modern Apprentice (MA) vacancies. (See TEC/LEC below.)

TECs/LECs (Training and Enterprise Councils/Local Enterprise Councils): local business partnerships have details of all the MA schemes. If they feel you are suitable, they will introduce you to an employer. If you get a place as a Modern Apprentice, you will be paid, continue your education and improve your interpersonal skills through key skill training.

Careers fairs: these promotional events – sometimes called the 'milk round' – are held mainly in colleges and universities. The purpose is for a diverse range of employers from many industries to promote their management training and business placement schemes to students. Your careers office can tell you what's available.

Internet: this is becoming a very popular source of information. Many retailers have dedicated websites. The sites vary in detail, but many contain company facts and figures as well as job opportunities, including training schemes. Some also have motivational questionnaires that you are invited to complete to see if you might be suitable for them. Trade organisations, recruitment specialists and government agencies may also have relevant information in their websites. If you don't have personal access to the Internet, then it would be worth using a friend's or accessing one at a cybercafé or the library. However, you must remember that you will have to pay for the time you are on the Internet.

Public libraries: they have a careers section and resources including photocopiers, access to databanks, and the Internet can be used for a fee. Depending on the size of library, it can be extremely useful for researching.

Job centres: many retailers advertise local vacancies here for a range of opportunities, from general assistants to managers. If you have few academic qualifications or want work experience, your job centre could be very useful.

Employment/recruitment agencies: these are found in most high streets. They may be generalist or focus on an occupational area, such as retailing, or a profession, such as accountancy. Some recruitment agencies advertise in the press on behalf of clients and may also keep registers of people who are looking for work.

Advertisements: whilst people often think of an advertisement as the best place to start job seeking, it isn't necessarily the case. Only about 20% of job vacancies are filled via advertisements. Retailers advertise on their own premises, in newspapers and trade press and journals. There are many journals and these usually focus on a specific areas within a sector. For example, if you want to work in fashion, *The Grocer* will not be a source of jobs for you. Publications are detailed in specialist directories which you can find in your local library.

Trade agencies and professional organisations: these can be excellent sources of information. They can provide literature, advice on academic routes and may also give an insight into where skill shortages exist. Some of these are listed in *Want to find out more?* on page 79.

Personal contacts and networking: a high percentage of jobs come from this source and it is particularly useful if you are thinking of making a career change. It is surprising how many useful contacts you didn't know you had! Telling someone you are looking for a change, work experience or a training scheme can often be enough. 'I can't help, but I know someone who can' can lead to, if not the world, then your first step on the retailing ladder.

Speculative approaches: there is nothing to stop you from making a direct approach to an organisation. An application will have more effect if you link it to something that is happening within the organisation – growth, new openings or takeovers. If you want to get on a training scheme, you may have to make a direct approach initially in order to get an application form.

Once you have explored your chosen area of retailing, the next stage is to apply for a job.

Applying for a job

Unless you have very powerful contacts, or your skills are so advanced that you are headhunted, you will have to make a formal application for a job. In the early stages, this will involve completing an application form or submitting your CV (curriculum vitae) to the organisation you are interested in.

This first stage is crucial! Your application and covering letter are the initial points of contact with prospective employers, so it is important that you get them right. As we pointed out earlier, one job advertisement can stimulate hundreds of responses, most of which will be rejected almost immediately. Employers don't have the time or resources to interview everybody who wants to work for them, so they will be ruthless in weeding out any applications that do not meet their selection criteria. The first stage for them is a screening process.

> 'We get so many applications for the management training scheme it is impossible to look at them in depth at this first stage. We have a set of criteria for scanning the applications related to academic achievements, work experience and leadership positions held.'
>
> *Recruitment manager, department store*

Organisations may have dedicated forms for specific purposes.

> Tesco uses a variety of forms: one for those seeking an industrial placement, another for A level or experienced management applicants, yet another for graduates and a different one for general applicants.

The Insider guide to completing application forms

Do:

- take your time: you cannot expect to complete an application form well if you try to fill it in during a spare half hour
- read through the form and the instructions carefully and fully

- photocopy the form and complete a draft in pencil before you even think about starting to complete the original
- make sure you do *exactly* what you are asked to do. (If you are asked to list your education in chronological order, start with secondary school and work through to your most recent college or university course, if applicable. If it asks for details of past employment in reverse chronological order, begin with your most recent job)
- answer the questions honestly: don't make claims you cannot substantiate
- get your facts straight. (Check dates, particularly for periods of education and employment, and don't leave unexplained gaps)
- print or write legibly in the requested colour and style: if they want a blue ballpoint pen use one. (Application forms may be photocopied numerous times by the selectors, and lilac, silver or green ink do not come through clearly: neither do they look professional)
- check your spelling, grammar and punctuation: better still, get somebody else to check them for you
- emphasise achievements and highlight relevant skills where appropriate. (Always try to give evidence of your skills and achievements. Employers want to know what you have done and can do now, not just what you think you can do)
- use sections such as 'Any other information' and 'Skills and experience' to sell yourself
- get permission from any referees before you give their names
- submit the form promptly, in an A4 or A5 envelope (unless one is supplied): make sure it is posted before the closing date
- keep a record of the finished application, together with the date of submission and where you have sent it: you may need to chase it up if you don't hear anything within the agreed timescales.

Don't:

- leave questions unanswered: write 'not applicable' (N/A) against those that don't apply to you
- put 'see CV' against questions, even if you are attaching this document. (One of the purposes of the application form is to enable an organisation to compare 'like with like', i.e. candidate information presented in the same way)
- give specific information on the salary you want. (Say 'to be discussed at interview' or 'negotiable'.)

'We have found that simply not following instructions or basic errors may ruin applicants' chances at the outset: using an inappropriate pen (fluorescent pink or gentian violet), typing instead of writing, leaving sections blank and forgetting to record vital statistics such as name or address!'

Recruitment manager, department store

The Insider guide to writing effective CVs

A CV can be a vital tool for anyone who is looking for a job. There are few absolutes for CVs: it is a personal brochure for selling yourself and so it should reflect you and the image you want to project. Your CV is particularly important if you are making a speculative approach to an organisation, going through an agency or networking (a proactive process of using friends, relations and colleagues to make potential contacts in your chosen industry).

Do:

- keep a record of any information that could be relevant to a job application. Use this as the basis of your CV
- follow the same advice as for application forms – give evidence to support any claims you make about your skills and experience
- keep your CV to a reasonable length: two pages of A4 paper should be sufficient. If it is much longer, you may be including irrelevant information
- type your CV, or get someone to type it for you

- run off a copy and check the spelling, punctuation and grammar
- use good quality (90-100gm), white, unlined paper for the final copy: it should be letter quality from an inkjet or laser printer
- use clear, jargon-free language and words in their simplest form.

Don't:
- rely on computer software to proofread the document for you
- think you can send the same CV out for every job for which you apply. Different employers demand different qualities from their staff and you should tailor your CV to meet the needs of any job specification you receive
- bind the document – this is unnecessary, particularly if potential employers want to make photocopies
- include photographs unless specifically requested.

Explore different styles for your CV. If you are just leaving school, college or university, then a straightforward chronological account of your education and work experience, together with some information on your interests and any responsible positions you have held, will be sufficient.

> 'I knew that getting my CV right was very important: I had to make sure it would be noticed so I read everything I could about drawing it up. I also had help from my form tutor, who was very supportive. After that, although I usually had to fill in application forms, my CV was a good source of information for the forms.'
>
> *Sales assistant, superstore*

On the other hand, if you are changing careers, then employers will be more interested in your employment record, so this section should be near the beginning.

> 'I thought that all I needed to do was identify my previous responsibilities. I soon learned that it was more important to identify my achievements and make sure I put in figures and facts to support these. A friend told me to remember that 'an employer wants to know what you achieved, not what you were supposed to do'.
>
> *Supervisor, superstore*

There are dozens of good books on the market that will help you to develop an effective CV. Buying one could be a useful investment – or borrow a copy from the library. However, beware of those that primarily focus on CVs for the North American market, unless you intend working in that part of the world. Whilst many of the principles are the same, there are differences in style of presentation.

The Insider guide to writing effective covering letters

In the distant past, it was common practice to send a very cursory covering letter, i.e. one that just referred to the advertisement, date and any attachments. Things are different now. You must include an effective covering letter with any application you make. This should:

- have a heading: identifying the job for which you are applying
- include an introductory paragraph: identifying where you heard about the vacancy. Employers use this information to monitor the success of their recruitment campaigns
- explain why you think you are a suitable candidate for the job. This should be two or three short paragraphs highlighting areas of experience or relevant skills you have mentioned in your CV or application form
- end with a closing paragraph in which you invite further contact from the employer.

If you want to make a speculative application, always try to get a named contact before you start: telephone the head office, ask for the personnel department and get the name of the appropriate person to whom you should write. At the same time, try to get any additional information about what they are looking for in new staff and how the company structures its selection process. If the organisation has a website, see if you can pick up any information from that.

The Insider guide to performing well at interviews

If an organisation thinks you have the skills, qualifications and experience they need, you will be called for an interview or asked to take part in an assessment centre, depending on their selection procedures.

Interviews are a two-way process. They help the employer to find out if you are the best person for the job, and they help you to decide if this is the job for you.

For you, the interview is a selling opportunity and you must convince the interviewer to buy you. You cannot do that without proper preparation. Making an effort builds your confidence and will impress your interviewer. Practising your interview skills can go a long way towards ensuring your success.

Here is a very brief guide to good interview techniques. If you are just starting on your career, haven't experienced many interviews or feel your skills are stale and could do with some dusting and polishing, invest in a book on interview techniques. There are many books available on the market that offer useful and detailed advice to help you improve your communication skills – some of which are specifically focused on interviewing.

The interview isn't just a physical meeting on the day: it is also a process of research and preparation.

Prepare, prepare, prepare...

- If you haven't already done so, research the organisation: get a set of reports and accounts and up-to-date literature from the company or the library, and check Internet websites.
- Read up on the company's directors, products, growth and problem areas, structure and mission.
- Find out as much as possible about the post you want (or training scheme you hope to join): get the job description (an outline of the programme). What does the work (programme) involve? How will your experience and skills help you meet the demands of the job? After all, the employers will want to see what you can do for them!

- Make sure that you know where the interview is and how to get there, its accessibility via public transport or if there is parking available if you want to drive.
- Think about the questions you might be asked: draw up a list of these together with constructive answers. Can you produce evidence to support any statements you make about what you can do? We can all claim to be good leaders: the selectors will want an example of when and how you demonstrated leadership skills.
- Think about the questions you want to ask; the interview is also a time for you to collect information.
- Practise being interviewed: use a tape recorder or video camera; ask a friend to role play with you or practise by yourself in front of a mirror.
- Find out the format of the interview: will it be with one person or a panel? Do you have to take any tests? How long will the whole process take?

On the day

- First impressions are lasting impressions: they *do* count! Wear appropriate clothes and check that you are well-groomed. Dressing for success may be a cliché, but your appearance is important and is something on which you will be judged.
- Set out early to arrive punctually. Give yourself plenty of time to cope with rush-hour traffic and train delays. If you have an interview first thing in the morning and have some distance to travel, think about travelling the night before and staying over.

Do:

- communicate your confidence through your body language: use eye contact to create rapport and confidence; walk and sit with your shoulders back and your head held up; look at people when you talk to them and they speak to you; smile
- listen to the questions and don't interrupt: how else will you find out what the selector wants to know?
- take your time when you answer questions – paraphrase what has been asked, if necessary

- give evidence, evidence and more evidence: support every claim you make with facts
- be honest: don't make claims about your talents you cannot support
- give a short, simple, positive answer if you are asked to talk about a difficult time in your career
- find out what happens next: how long will you have to wait to hear the decision?

Don't:

- answer yes or no: use the opportunity to make a positive point
- apologise for yourself: it is your maturity and ability to do the job that count
- *ever* criticise a previous boss, company or tutor
- argue if you disagree with the interviewer's views: support your own views constructively
- be frightened of silence
- descend to someone else's standards of incompetence or ungraciousness.

The Insider guide to performing well at assessment centres

An assessment centre is not a place you go to for your interview, but the process whereby employers can take a detailed look at prospective candidates to find out more about their skills and aptitudes and thus their suitability for a job or a training scheme. It is a thorough way of analysing candidates favoured by large organisations and companies which regularly recruit potential management and management staff.

Assessment centres vary in format and duration. You may be asked to participate in a one-day session at head office, spend two days at a residential centre or spend some time in a store. You may find yourself working on a committee, taking part in a role play, giving a presentation, preparing a report or making constructions out of sticky backed paper. Most, or all, of these activities will have a retailing bias: the overall purpose will be to see how you might fit into the industry. You could also be asked to sit aptitude tests covering aspects of numeracy and communication. All this, and interviews too!

'We run assessment centres if we are recruiting for management posts or staffing new stores. Candidates have an interview, carry out observed exercises related to commercial and visual skills, a prioritising exercise and complete a series of personality tests. New store staff do a morning of observed work in one of our stores.

We also put all our potential management trainees through an assessment centre – A level, graduates and business placement students. The format is similar – a 30-minute structured interview, three retail-related group exercises and personality tests. They also present a report they have prepared previously on a subject we have given them.'

Regional manager, ladies' fashions

Throughout the proceedings, you will be observed by trained assessors who will be looking for evidence of organisational skills, leadership ability, communication and decision-making skills, as well as evaluating your ability to work in a team and motivate others.

'At first I found it a bit unnerving, but after I while I began to relax and enjoy the assessment centre – it was fun working with other participants to solve retailing problems. At the end, it was good getting feedback on where I performed well and what areas would need to be strengthened during my traineeship.'

Sales manager designate, department store

If you have to attend an assessment centre:

- be willing to take part, even if you think that some of the exercises are more appropriate to the schoolroom. These activities all have a purpose and the assessors know what they are looking for
- work with the rest of your group. Even though you all may be competing for the same job, you will not gain points through being aggressively competitive. Teamwork is the buzzword of today's workplace
- don't take over or try to dominate your group. Be prepared to listen as well as talk

- enjoy yourself – assessment centres can be a lot of fun – but don't get carried away. Completing a two-day course with a hangover is difficult and assessors often save the most difficult task until last.

Work experience

If you are just about to start your career, then a period of work experience can be an invaluable way of finding out if you have chosen the right field of employment. Work experience has become an integral part of secondary school education: it not only allows students to find out more about different jobs, it also educates them in the harsh realities of working life.

> 'Retailing was never my first choice because I thought it was going to be all shelf filling. I wanted to do my work experience in a leisure centre – but so did most of my pals. I had to take one of the placements that were available at a local supermarket. Surprisingly, I did like it – I liked working with customers, got on well with the people in my team and I learned quite a lot – and while I was there, I didn't fill any shelves. I got a part-time job with them whilst I was doing an art course at college. When I left, I decided to forget the art and go into full-time retailing, and here I am now at 21: a stock control manager for one of the big food multiples.'
> *Stock control manager, supermarket*

Whilst at school or 6th form college, students can continue work experience in the GNVQs (General National Vocational Qualifications) in distribution services – at foundation, intermediate or advanced level.

Part-time/vacation work

The need for some ready cash has encouraged many young people to take part-time and vacation work. Consequently, most students have some experience of work before they take the plunge and apply for their first permanent job. Getting part-time or temporary work in retailing can be relatively easy: stores are opening for longer hours, employers are employing fewer full-time staff and going over to more flexible arrangements – part time, weekend only, evenings only. Staff are needed to fill all types of positions with a range of hours. Whether you are looking for work experience, part-time or vacation work, employers will be expecting you to have certain skills and attributes. At the very least, you will need to be reasonably articulate, with a clean, neat appearance and have an interest in retailing.

> 'When I was in 6th form college doing my A levels, I got a Saturday job in high street shop. Although I had been thinking about hotel management and catering, working in the shop helped me to make my mind up that fashion retailing was what I wanted.'
>
> *Sales manager, ladies' fashion*

General entry

> 'We are not looking for budding Einsteins, but we do need applicants who are bright, articulate, organised and with an interest in customers and selling.'
>
> *Store manager, superstore*

As mentioned before, retailing is an open industry where committed individuals can get on without necessarily having achieved high academic qualifications. However, employers will be looking for a range of skills and aptitudes, including the ability to work in a team, good communication, energy and an interest in retailing and customers. Could you work co-operatively with colleagues? Can you make yourself understood? Are you reasonably fit, will you enjoy customer contact and get a buzz from retailing?

One of the key features of a successful job application is the ability to provide evidence that supports your claims. Anybody can walk into an interview and say that they are good with people, love working with others as a team and have plenty of energy. What the selector wants to see is evidence of these skills.

During your time in education, or in part-time or vacation jobs, you will have started to develop a skills base. Use this checklist to identify things you have done that show you possess the required skills.

Skill/aptitude	Y/N	What is my evidence?
Have you the ability to work in a team?		Committee work, team sports, group projects, voluntary/community work
Are you a good communicator?		Discussion/debating groups, work with special needs groups, leading/chairing a group, acting as a spokesperson
Do you have plenty of energy?		Extra-curricular activities such as voluntary work, active sports/hobbies, organising events
Are you interested in retailing (fashion/books/ food...)?		Work experience, part-time or vacation work in the industry/sector, projects, awareness of current fashion trends/authors/healthy eating
Do you enjoy customer contact?		Work experience/part-time or vacation work in a service industry, voluntary/committee work, group activities.

Can you motivate staff and could you deal with customers? We want ambitious people with drive, leadership, unbounded energy and a creative ability.

Department store advertisement

If you are contemplating a career change, retailing experience isn't always needed – even if you want to start on the management ladder. It is more important that you demonstrate people management skills, interpersonal effectiveness and business management skills: these skills are relatively easily transferred from one industry to another. Have you managed a team of people effectively? Are you confident, assertive and able to deal with problems? Are you commercially minded and do you strive to achieve personal and team goals?

You will need to give evidence of your various skills and relate them to what the advertisement or the company literature is asking for.

'When I was promoted, I had to manage a team which included people who were twice my age. At first this was very daunting, but now it is a very happy, well-motivated team. This has been proved by our most recent returns – we have exceeded target for the last two months.'

Department head, supermarket

Management trainee entry

You can progress more quickly in retailing if you have higher academic qualifications and can get on a 'fast-track' training scheme. Many retailers offer recruits a variety of places on work experience and management training programmes, with a view to them being their 'managers of the future'. The aim is to attract some of the most suitable recruits who are capable of achieving store management positions within five years or less.

Vacation and gap year placements

Some students want to take a year out before university. Many travel or do voluntary work, but many others may have to spend their gap year in full-time employment to generate funds for the expense that follows or to get a taste of an industry. Some retailers now offer a gap year placement in retail, logistics, IT or marketing. Students have to give evidence that they have a deferred place on a relevant degree course. Retailers hope that the right students will enjoy this experience enough to apply for a training scheme.

A variety of business placements are available to undergraduates, ranging from short vacation periods (6-12 weeks) to a full year. The content and format of these programmes differs widely, but students on a short placement will get a taster of a wide range of jobs – selling, handling goods, working in a team. On a longer placement, students will follow a structured programme of work experience and job shadowing, and they will carry out project work to give them an insight into retailing, strengthen their personal and business skills, and create a project of value to the business and the students. They may also get sponsorship for the final year of their degree. This is another way for retailers to 'capture' the interest of students and attract the managers of the future.

> 'I did a retail management degree and spent my third year with a food-retailing organisation. During this time, I learned an incredible amount about myself, the business of retailing and the organisation. The company took me on to their graduate management scheme when I left university. I am a manager now, and the company is sponsoring me through my Retailing MBA – all of this because of my sandwich placement.'
>
> *Operations controller, supermarket*

Trainee programmes

In Part One, we pointed out that these schemes range from those accepting trainees with GCSEs in Maths and English plus relevant experience, up to graduates. The majority of the well-known operators run either graduate only (requiring a 2:2 degree as minimum) or graduate and a separate A level scheme (usually a minimum of two As necessary). Competition is extremely keen for any of these structured programmes. Retailers know they can be choosy, so you will need to work hard to get a place.

> Debenhams gets more than 5,500 applications for around 120 management and 30 business placements each year, whilst Marks & Spencer attracts more than 10,000 hopefuls for approximately 350 places.

On the application form, as well as the usual questions about your education and work experience, you will have more detailed sections to complete. The questions vary but you can anticipate some which ask you to demonstrate a number of personal skills:

- Describe a situation in which you had to persuade others to accept your view: what were the circumstances and what did you do?
- Describe a situation where you have worked successfully in a team on a project or activity: how did you do to contribute to the success?

- Describe a situation where you had to overcome difficulties to achieve a goal: what were the problems and what did you do?

Trainees usually have two or three 'hoops' to go through. First, a structured interview; second, an aptitude test and, third an assessment centre. Some organisations delay the aptitude test and combine this with the assessment centre. During the assessment centre, applicants will be expected to show evidence of a wide range of skills and aptitudes – many of these have been mentioned previously. Others are leadership, analytical ability, accepting responsibility and a wide range of interpersonal skills. Retailers invest large sums in their 'managers of the future', so they need to be certain that those they select have the right potential.

'What we will be looking for is evidence that they can be creative, offer ideas and suggestions, network with the others in the group, be an individual and be prepared to take ownership for their own development. We also expect them to be able "think the big picture" – particularly the graduates.'

Recruitment manager, department store

A consortium of leading food and non-food retailers, Cortco Associates, has identified a range of competencies they will expect their graduate trainees to demonstrate very quickly. At the interview and assessment stage, applicants will be expected to show that they have some of the required competencies and have the potential to achieve the rest. The Cortco Competencies are listed on the following pages.

Find out what training programmes are available using some of the suggestions we made at the beginning of this section. Once you have identified the scheme (or schemes), get a named contact with whom you can liaise.

Personal effectiveness

Personal presence: having a positive impact. Setting high standards for your own work and expecting to succeed through tenacity, drive and commitment.

Emotional resilience: bouncing back quickly from setbacks. Learning from experience – including mistakes, prepared to be proactive, coping under pressure.

Assertiveness: acting and communicating with others in a confident manner. Expressing opinions, which are influenced by personal convictions, and defending them when challenged. Demonstrating independence.

Self-confidence: having belief in one's *own* ability and judgement. Behaving in an open and honest way, a self-starter, who is able to admit to mistakes, take as well as give criticism and actively influence events.

Task management: completes tasks in the most effective and efficient way. Getting the job done is important. Doesn't give up easily, tries to solve problems rather than postpone them, and recognises the importance of deadlines and timescales.

Flexibility/adaptability: responds promptly and effectively to changes. Coping with planned or unexpected change and developments, modifying behaviour if necessary, in order to achieve a goal.

Self-development: seeks to improve own performance. Taking responsibility for own performance, reviewing experiences and seeking new activities to learn from. Positively encouraging feedback.

Managing people and working with others

(interpersonal skills and people management)

Team working and awareness: willing and able to participate as a full member of the team. Encouraging contributions, actively listening to others, and participating even when the subject or task will not deliver personal gain. Taking actions that indicate recognition of one's own impact, and take account of the feelings and needs of others in order to build a working relationship.

Team leading: showing the ability to guide, direct and motivate individuals or groups to task accomplishment. Offering support; taking ownership quickly; prepared to accept responsibility on issues and be judged on them, not passing the buck. Shaping the outcome of the group's output.

Communication skills: adopting an appropriate style, tone and language to inform and influence. Delivering all communication clearly and accurately with an appreciation of the need to always check the receiver's understanding. An awareness of the range of skills and techniques involved with both written and spoken communication, including non-verbal indicators.

Managing and coaching for performance: demonstrating the ability to improve the skills and performance of others. Giving and finding opportunities for others to develop. Explaining clearly the objectives which are being set, checking that what is required and why are appreciated. Delegating, giving feedback and support, mentoring and managing expectations are important elements.

Organisational ability and creative thinking

Planning and organising: establishing a course of action for oneself and/or others to accomplish a specific goal, involving both the short and long term. Requires an ability to prioritise, the monitoring of progress, and benchmarking to check progress. Reviewing the completed task to gain insights for next cycle.

Forward planning: developing clear and logical step-by-step plans for self and others. Setting out what needs to happen, how and when, with what.

Critical thinking and analytical consideration: knowing the problem, getting facts/data before applying judgement. Gathering relevant information, identifying issues, sifting and sorting complex information, effectively analysing data and situations; and then applying logic to draw conclusions and solve the problem.

Decisiveness: readiness to make decisions, act or commit oneself.

Innovation and strategic thinking: is enquiring, and has the ability to grasp new concepts quickly. Demonstrating an ability to think laterally and 'outside the box', producing innovative and creative solutions.

Business focus: attributes possessed by successful retail managers.

Customer focus: understanding and anticipating the needs of the customer. Seeking to encourage customer loyalty, an awareness of customer trends.

Commercialism and business awareness: understands the retail business environment. Seeing how new events and situations will affect the organisation, understanding the nature and effects of competition and what is important to the bottom line.

Job motivation: enjoys and is motivated by the buzz of retail. Retail managerial activities and responsibilities provide and maintain interest and deliver job satisfaction.

GETTING ON

As with most jobs, your prospects for promotion are dependent on your ability and performance. If you have started your career as a general applicant and want to move up the career ladder, you will probably be expected to take national vocational qualifications or study part time for industry-related qualifications. Some of these are detailed on page 69 – the list is not exhaustive!

> 'Since I have been promoted to supervisor, I have been on a number of management courses and hope to take my level 3 Retailing NVQ. I have put myself forward to be trained as an assessor. I am considering some distance-learning programmes to improve my prospects further. I hope to be an assistant or deputy manager within two years.'
>
> *Senior sales, ladies' fashion*

If you want to work your way to a management level, or you are on a management training scheme, you will probably be expected to be mobile. A number of the bigger retailers now operate beyond the UK, in Europe and as far afield as the Far East. You could be expected to move to an operation in one of these locations. Being prepared to move gives you more opportunities to gain experience in different environments and locations whilst moving onwards and upwards. It also gives the organisation the chance to 'juggle' its human resources more effectively. If you are asked to move, you may be given temporary accommodation for a limited period or receive a resettlement grant or relocation assistance.

> 'For three of our programmes – store management, personnel and training, and finance operations management – we ask for national mobility. Trainees could be placed in their home town for their initial training. The earlier they apply the better their chance of getting a place nearer their home town or university.'
>
> *Recruitment manager, department store*

If you decide to stay in one place, you could reduce your opportunities for promotion.

> 'My personal circumstances are such that I don't want to move. This means I am unlikely to get further promotion as I run the biggest department in the store. But, I love the job and am happy as I am.'
> *Sales manager, department store*

Retailers believe in promoting from within. Vacancies within an organisation will often be advertised internally. If you are ambitious and keen to succeed in your career, you will keep abreast of any opportunities.

You should also be willing to take as much training as you can handle to develop your skills. Whilst you will be expected to manage your own self-learning, both on-job and off-job training will be an integral part of your development – particularly when you take on new responsibilities and roles. You must be flexible, adaptable and meet new challenges face on. Talk to your line manager (or personnel officer, if appropriate) about opportunities that could be open to you.

> 'I gave up my well-paid administration job to move south. My savings were dwindling so I took the job – I didn't really want to work in a shop! I really began to love the job, the atmosphere – very busy – lots of hustle and bustle, staff working as a team, having specific responsibilities.
> After three months, I sat down with my manager to find out about prospects within the company and she outlined what was available. Two months later, I was promoted. I didn't have previous qualifications – but it was more about the person, being willing to learn and being committed, than about academic achievements.
> I have done many courses, such as train the trainer, visual display, legal issues and team building. We have training 3-4 times per year. I have taken my retailing NVQ and I am a NVQ assessor. I have also done self-development projects at head office. They help to identify other areas I may enjoy if I want to move from the shop floor.'
> *Store manager, ladies' fashion*

Retailing qualifications

A variety of qualifications are available depending on the retailing area, the organisation and individual roles. Most of the following are 'open', i.e. you do not need specific academic qualifications to undertake them. However, they are, in the main, competence based and ideally should be undertaken when in employment.

Scottish/National Vocational Qualifications (work-based qualifications) range from level 1 to level 5, covering:

- retail operations
- distribution and warehousing operations
- floristry
- retail sales delivery
- visual merchandising
- home shopping
- mail operations
- meat and poultry butchery operations
- procurement
- training and development
- customer service
- administration
- distributive operations
- bakery service
- craft making
- pharmacy services
- management
- strategic management
- operational management
- owner management.

Other college-based qualifications include:

BDS Certificate and Diploma (British Display Society)

BTEC National Diploma in Design (Display)

Diploma in Professional Bookselling

BTEC First, National and Higher National Certificate and Diploma: Retail Management

BTEC Higher National Certificate in Business (Retail Management)

Foundation Certificate in Management (Accredited by Manchester Metropolitan University)

City and Guilds in Retailing.

Management trainees

If you are accepted on to a management trainee programme, you will be put through a structured course designed to give you the broadest experience and training in a relatively short period of time. Training programmes vary in length, depending on the specialism – financial, buying, catering, etc. – but can last up to two years. Programmes are constantly evolving in style and content, but if you are on a general retail management programme, you can expect some of the following experiences:

- **induction training:** a combination of in-store and residential. Store-specific induction will include clarification of terms and conditions and provide information fundamental to your role. It may include a period of job shadowing the store manager and management team, and will give you an idea of the work you will be undertaking. Residential induction will be with other trainees to help you establish a network, explain the scheme in more detail and offer an insight into the culture and strategy of the organisation
- **off-job training:** courses to help you to develop skills in areas such as coaching, managing time, managing performance and appraisal and leadership. These will improve specific areas of your knowledge and expertise
- **placements:** on the shop floor to gain practical experience and skills, and in head office to gain an understanding of all aspects of the business
- **monthly reviews:** to enable you and the organisation to assess your performance and how well you are achieving your objectives.

During your training, you will be allocated a mentor, a member of staff who will be there to support and advise you throughout the programme. You will also have support and training from line management and personnel.

'I have really enjoyed the programme and, of course, am delighted now that I have my first posting. I have had very good support from my current store manager who has always been there to help with a problem. I also had a very good mentor throughout.'
Ex-graduate trainee, department store

In the initial stages, some of the work may surprise you – it may seem quite mundane, particularly if you see yourself as a high flier. However, one of the best ways of learning is by doing and in retailing everyone works as a team. You will have a better appreciation of how the big wheel works if you have sampled some of the 'cog' roles. In retailing, no job is too menial, no matter who you are.

'During my training I have had lots of placements – menswear, casuals and supervisor on the loading bay night shift over Christmas. The blokes didn't take to a girl being in charge – I coped by almost becoming one of the lads and proving I could do the job well. I unloaded, stayed longer, pulled weight and earned respect for it.'
Ex-graduate trainee, department store

Once you have successfully completed your training, you will take responsibility for your own development. You will be expected to draw up a personal development plan which identifies your short- and long-term goals.

'Trainees must understand that it is not all going to be handed to them on a plate – they have to go out and get the training or development.'
Recruitment manager, department store

Once you have identified your goals and the company feels they fit in with their overall objectives and strategy, you will need to identify how you will achieve them. It could be through experience, training courses and/or further academic undertakings.

'The company will be sponsoring me to do my IPD (Institute of Personnel and Development) qualification and, as this department is very busy, I will probably do this through their flexible learning system. I will need to be very motivated for that, but having had a rigorous training programme, I don't think that will be a problem.'
Personnel officer, department store head office

It has been mentioned already, but if you are not working in a head office operation and want to progress up the management ladder, you will need to be prepared to move around the country.

> 'When I joined the scheme, I knew I would have to move about if I wanted to progress. Already I have been in four locations – and that is in only three years. With the exception of my initial training, each move has been a promotion, so at the rate I am going, I should be a manager of my own department store soon, and that could be back in one of my earlier postings!'
>
> *Ex-graduate trainee, department store*

The following qualifications may be undertaken by graduates as appropriate:

CIMA exams (The Chartered Institute of Management Accountancy)

CIM Certificate, Advanced Certificate and Postgraduate Diploma (The Chartered Institute of Marketing)

BA in Retail Management

Certificate in Food and Grocery Industry Management (post graduate).

GETTING OUT

So, you are in one sector of retailing, but you decide it's not for you – what is your next step? You have certain skills. Are they transferable? If so to what, and where?

Opportunities exist in both the food and non-food sectors and careers tend to follow through in one rather than the other. But, in these days of multi-skilling (training individuals to carry out a variety of tasks across a wide area), there is no reason why someone should not be able to move fairly easily from food to non-food and vice versa.

'I was working in the non-food sector – as manager in a DIY retailing operation. I felt there was no future there and I needed a career change. I got this job through a specialist agency, as I liked the idea of the fast nature of food retailing. My role is customer service manager and I aim to be a store manager in a year. I never intend to leave stores – I don't want to be an area manager – I want a big, large turnover, central London store. If I did leave, I would go to another food retailer.'

Customer services manager, superstore

Whilst there can be fewer opportunities the higher up the ladder you climb, the management skills you have gained are likely to be more easily transferable.

'My prospects are limited here. Having just been promoted, there is only one other upward training job – I don't think I want a sideways move, as I am unsure about working in personnel. My experience in training can be transferred to many organisations. In four to five years' time, if I don't stay here, I would like to move into one of the 'blue chip' computer companies. I also want to get Europe on my CV at some stage.'

Training and development controller, department store

'The higher up the ladder one gets, the more limited the opportunities are – it is, after all, a pyramid which is narrower at the top. There could be opportunities for me in other parts of the group, but, realistically, my next move will be external to the company. In the longer term, therefore, what I would like to do is run my own business – use some of the general management and 'people' skills I have developed to move into a different industry, such as consultancy. I really enjoy retailing but there is a burn-out factor.'

Area manager, ladies' fashion

Conclusion

'Our job is to make the customer feel valued.'

Store manager, ladies' fashion

Every role in retailing – whether in a convenience store, a fashion outlet or a group's head office – is focused on delivering what the customer wants. If you don't like customers then you shouldn't do the job.

> 'You must be able to work with others – in retailing you cannot work alone. You have to be there for each other. It is very demanding and challenging and to do it right needs a large balance of different skills.'
>
> *Sales manager, department store*

You must be prepared to work in a team to achieve goals. If you are at the 'sharp end' then the pace can be fast and frenetic – particularly in food retailing, where the throughput of customers is high.

> 'Retailers work very hard and they are there all the time to please people – this can be very difficult on occasions.'
>
> *Department controller, superstore*

The hours may be unsociable, the tasks repetitive and your feet may get sore, but if you are committed and prepared to work hard, the rewards can be good – regardless of your academic background.

> 'Retailing is very undervalued and unrecognised as a career, but it offers very good careers in an exciting sector.'
>
> *Personnel director, men's and ladies' wear multiple*

Whilst retailing has changed enormously over the years – and it continues to change – it can make for an exciting and challenging career.

JARGON BUSTER

Anchor store
The main store, or stores, around which a shopping mall is built.

Blue-chip organisation
Technically, one whose shares are a reliable investment, but the term is often used to refer to a respected, solid organisation.

Competencies
Skills or attributes that show someone is able to do something, such as analysing a situation.

Convenience store
Small stores selling a mixture of products, but mainly food and drink.

Department store
These stores usually have a large floor space on a number of floors. Some sections are franchised.

Do-it-yourself scanning
A hand-held machine for customers to price products and prepare their own bill.

Electronic funds transfer (EFTPOS)
Systems such as Delta or Switch for accessing customers' funds.

Fmcg (fast-moving consumer goods) industry
An industry where the turnover of goods is very quick.

Franchised operations
A method used by designer houses and other retailers to hire space in a department store through which to market their goods.

Frontline staff
Those people who have direct contact with customers, such as checkout operators.

Getting the big picture
Getting an overview rather than looking at individual parts – for example with a problem.

Independents
One-off operations.

Laser scanner
A machine for reading the barcode on products to identify prices and coding.

Mixed goods retailing
Classification for operations with a variety of goods on sale.

Mixed goods store
These sell a range of goods, from household equipment to confectionery.

Multiple
An operation with more than two stores.

Niche specialist
A retailer who sells one type of product range only.

One-stop shopping
The concept that customers are able to do all their shopping either in one store or in stores grouped together, as in a shopping mall.

Out-of-town sites
Large retail sites located on the outskirts of urban areas.

Own label
Products – usually produced by a leading manufacturer – sold with the retailer's identity.

Personal shoppers
Individuals dedicated to assisting customers with specific purchases – usually in department stores.

Retail parks
Large areas housing a variety of retailers, such as electrical, furniture and carpet and DIY operations – all superstores.

Sharp-end operations
A term used by large retail operations to refer to those working in their stores (as opposed to behind the scenes).

Shopping malls
Covered purpose-built operations housing a variety of stores in a range of sizes, with facilities such as car parks, restaurants, fast-food operations and entertainment.

Specialists
Retailers who specialise in one area, e.g. fashion.

Write-offs
Faulty garments or goods that cannot be sold (or re-sold) to customers.

Y2K
The year 2000.

WANT TO FIND OUT MORE?

Institute of Grocery Distribution (IGD)
Grange Lane
Letchmore Heath
Watford
Herts WD2 8DQ
Tel: 01923 857141
Fax: 01923 852531
e-mail:igd@igd.org.uk

Alliance of Independent Retailers and Businesses
Bank Chambers
5-9 St. Nicholas Street
Worcester WR1 1UW
Tel: 01905 612733
Fax: 01905 215010
www.indretailer.co.uk

Chartered Institute of Marketing
Moorhall
Cookham
Maidenhead
Berkshire
SL6 9QH
Tel: 01628 427500
Fax: 01628 427158
www.cim.co.uk

The Booksellers Association
Minster House
272 Vauxhall Bridge Road
London SW1V 1BA
Tel: 0171 834 5477
Fax: 0171 834 8812

British Display Society
70a Crayford High Street
Dartford DAl 4EF
Tel: 01322 550 544

Professional organisation for display.

The Distributive National Training Organisation (DNTO)
The Coda Centre
189 Munster Road
London SW6 6AW
Tel: 0171 386 5599
Fax: 0171 386 9599

The Government-recognised organisation responsible for the
education, training, qualifications and competitiveness of the
distributive industries.

British Institute of Retailing
The Hygeia Building
3rd Floor
66-68 College Road
Harrow
Middx HAl IFD
Tel: 0181 324 1609
Fax: 0181 324 1235

British Retail Consortium
5 Grafton Street
London W1X 3LB
Tel: 0171 647 1500
Fax: 0171 647 1599

Trade association with a membership of 90% of the retail industry.

Institute of Personnel and Development
IPD House
Camp Road
London SW19 4UX
Tel: 0181 971 9000
Fax: 0181 263 3333
www.ipd.co.uk

Distributive Industry Training Advisory Council (DITAC)/
British Shops and Stores Association
Middleton House
2 Main Road
Middleton Cheney
Banbury
Oxon OX17 2TN
Tel: 01295 712277
Fax: 01295 711358
www.di-net.co.uk

Trade and training association for the retail industry.

WANT TO READ ALL ABOUT IT?

Directories
Brad Directory (newspapers and journals), EMAP Media (published annually).

Benn's Media (newspapers and journals), Miller Freeman plc (published annually).

Which Subject? Which Career?, Consumer Association, 1996.

GET (university courses), published annually.

Careers Enclycopaedia, Cassell, 1997.

Booklets
Graduate careers information booklets, Association of Graduate Careers Advisory Services (AGCAS), CSU (published annually).

Your Career in Food Retailing and Wholesaling, Institute of Grocery Distribution.

Working in Retailing, Careers and Occupational Information Centre (COIC), Department for Education and Employment (DfEE), 1997.

Working in Marketing and Sales, COIC.

Working in Fashion, COIC.

Second Chances, COIC.

Books
Bede Cammock-Elliott, *Get a Life!* Industrial Society, 1994.

Mark Parkinson, *Interviews Made Easy*, Kogan Page, 1994.

Harry Tolley and Ken Thomas, *How to Pass Verbal Reasoning Tests*, Kogan Page, 1996.

Lyn Williams, *Readymade CVs*, Kogan Page, 1996.

Mark Parkinson, *How to Master Personality Questionnaires*, Kogan Page, 1997.

Marthe Sansgret and Dyane Adams, *Rate Yourself*, 2nd ed, Kogan Page, 1998.

Jim Barrett *Career, Aptitude and Selection Tests*, Kogan Page, 1998.

Helen Vandevelde, *Exploring Career Opportunities*, Trotman & Co Ltd, 1998.

Jo Gardiner, *Flying Start*, Industrial Society, 1999.

Debra Allcock, *High Flying*, Industrial Society, 1999.

Notes

The Insider Career Guides

Banking and the City
Karen Holmes
ISBN 1 85835 583 4

The Environment
Melanie Allen
ISBN 1 85835 588 5

Information and Communications Technology
Jacquetta Megarry
ISBN 1 85835 593 1

Retailing
Liz Edwards
ISBN 1 85835 578 8

Sport
Robin Hardwick
ISBN 1 85835 573 7

Travel and Tourism
Karen France
ISBN 1 85835 598 2

New titles
Watch out for three new insider guides coming out later in
1999 – the insider guide to successful job search (1 85835 815
9), the insider guide to interviews and other selection methods
(1 85835 820 5), and the insider guide to networking (1 85835
825 6).

These and other Industrial Society titles are available from
all good bookshops or direct from The Industrial Society on
telephone 0870 400 1000 (p&p charges apply).